21 Days of Poetry

Lucy Maiden

Presentation by *BookLeaf Publishing*

Web: www.bookleafpub.com

E-mail: info@bookleafpub.com

ISBN: 9789395950824

First edition 2022

DEDICATION

To my siblings, Alice and William, who inspired these poems with their unique personalities and loving hearts. I love you now and forever.

ACKNOWLEDGEMENT

Thank you to my amazing family who are always there for me during the highs and lows. Special thanks to Laura, my beautiful mother. You are always there for me no matter what and always love me. Nothing can describe my love and appreciation for you. To both of my dad's, Kyle and Jamie. Kyle, you always give me helpful guidance and give me everything you have to offer. Jamie, you always support my crazy ideas and help me achieve my goals. I love you two and you'll always be in my life no matter what.

When I Dream

When I dream, I can fly,
I flap my wings and so,
Flying high, above the sky,
Off the ground, off I go.

A Summers Day

The humid is near.
Fresh fruit blooming with glee.
See, summer is key.

Under the Sun

Taming the skies,
We're together.
I see it in your eyes,
We're connected by a tether.

You and I

When I walk, I fall,
when I dream, I run,
Your faint call,
I run to you.

Endless Love

5

Laughing and yelling,
I see you in the corner.
Our love never dies.

A Soft Smile

Looking across my shoulder,
I see you next to me,
I smile at you.
We're forever free.

Forever Trapped

Look over there, what do you see?
Twists and turns,
Here, the old gumtree,
They're suffering from ancient burns.

Stored Away

In my room, all alone.
I lived by myself,
All the love and happiness I got,
I laid up on the shelf.

More Heat and Love

9

A small group of friends,
Sitting around the fire,
More warmth than it.

Surrounded by Love

Feeling loved,
Surrounded by heat.
You're my beloved,
Making my heart beat.

Pearls in the Sky

Looking out the window,
This giant world.
Knowing it will be OK,
In the pearled sky.

Nothing to Separate

I'm in love with you.
You smile at me, I smile back.
Now and forever.

Bonding by the Ocean

Laughing with you,
On the blue ocean.
Water of blue,
Falling for the love potion.

Never Going to Cry

Loving myself,
Looking at the blue sky,
Fresh air in my lungs.
Never able to cry.

Self-confidence

15

Having confidence,
Feeling proud.
Stepping up,
To the endless crowd.

Perfect Already

You're amazing. Do
Not change yourself for me,
You're perfect as is.

What's a Friend?

A friend is someone,
That you can tell anything,
And trust them always.

I Hear It

In your arms,
I belong.
I hear your heart,
Like a beautiful song.

What It's Like

Loving you it's like,
A gift everyday.
But it's a surprise.

Missing You, Far Away

Wrapped in endless love,
With you it's a dream, but,
I'm missing you here.

Enough is Enough

Enough is enough,
Because I deserve better,
I say no, so stop.